PARTICIPANT'S GUIDE

STARTING OVER

YOUR LIFE BEYOND REGRETS

DAVE FERGUSON & JON FERGUSON

BIG IDEA
RESOURCES

Published in the United States by **Big Idea Resources**.

Printed in the United States of America
2016—First Edition
ISBN 978-0-692-75582-2

Special Sales for bulk purchases of this guide contact John Mantia at Solid Impressions at 630.543.7300 or john@solid-impressions.com.

We are grateful to Jon Hughes, and his team of writers at COMMUNITY, who ensured that this participant's guide, would be a practical resource to help many people live beyond their regrets! Thanks Jon!

CONTENTS

YOUR LIFE BEYOND REGRETS

INTRODUCTION

Regret is a universal experience. We all make wrong or foolish choices, or something happens to us, or someone hurts us, and we regret it. Sometimes we even start regretting a decision before we make it because we're so sure the consequences are going to disappoint us!

Some people have bigger regrets or dwell on their regrets more than others do, but everybody has them. So don't feel alone if you look back on some episodes of embarrassing bone-headedness or epic nastiness in your past and wish you could do it all over again.

Many of us deal with the regrets of ruined relationships, lost jobs, or failure at moments of golden opportunity. This series of small group discussions is for you if you have spent a night in jail, rejected good advice, or hurt somebody you cared about. This series is for all of us who have regrets of any type burdening our souls. Truthfully; it's for every one of us.

I bet your mind is already simmering with thoughts of your own regrets. They might be minor regrets that you can dismiss from your head whenever you want or major regrets that are painful and crippling and ever present to you. Maybe you even have a mega regret that you try to suppress beneath the surface of your consciousness. It feels like trying to hold a beach ball underwater, and it's exhausting isn't it?

The book ***Starting Over*** was written based on an observation my brother, Jon and I made shortly after the release of our previous book, ***Finding Your Way Back to God***. In that book we described a series of five awakenings that people go through if they feel that they have become distant from God and are finding their way back.

> Awakening to Longing—"There's got to be more."
> Awakening to Regret—"I wish I could start over."
> Awakening to Help—"I can't do this on my own."
> Awakening to Love—"God loves me deeply after all."
> Awakening to Life—"Now this is living!"

In our conversations with people who had read the book, we were pleased that what we had written resonated with so many people. But we noticed something curious: many of the people we talked to experienced the Awakening to Regret, but then got stuck there.

For example, one woman in her mid-thirties told us, "I wish I could start over after my divorce—I really do. But you have no idea how the break-up has affected the way I feel about myself. How lonely I am. What big financial trouble I'm in today. Not to mention the loss of my hopes for having children, which was my biggest dream. Honestly, I don't really see God as caring about me or having anything much good left for me."

Jon and I can't remember which of us first coined the term, but somewhere along the way we started using the phrase Sorry Cycle to describe what people meant when they said things like this. They were sorry about what happened and felt sorry for themselves, but they just couldn't seem to get beyond that. Essentially they were going from longing to regret, back to longing then regret, in an endless cycle of repetition.

They were stuck in their regrets.
Paralyzed.
And miserable because of it.

We've created this participant's guide to help you and others come face to face with your regrets, and learn to start over again. Consider this guide as a tool to keep at hand as you learn to live your life beyond regret alongside the members of your group. You will find in its pages everything you need for the next five weeks.

Each session will help you move one step closer to living beyond regrets.

Week 1 - Love Your Regrets
Week 2 - Recognize Your Regrets
Week 3 - Release Your Regrets
Week 4 - Redeem Your Regrets
Week 5 - Live Beyond Your Regrets

Whatever the magnitude of your regret, and whatever the cause, I have a word of hope for you:

This is not the end.

LOVE YOUR REGRETS

"You can start over"

SESSION 1 - LOVE YOUR REGRETS

Session 1 Big Idea:
Regrets. We all have them. It may be something you wish you hadn't done, or a missed opportunity where you didn't take action and wish that you had. It might be something that was done to you; you were the victim, yet you still feel regret.

Whether it's something from last week, last year, or decades ago, you long to make things right – to change direction, to begin again. Yet somehow your attempts to fulfill this longing elude you.

We call this constant back-and-forth between longing and regret the "Sorry Cycle." It's a pattern many of us live with every day.

The surprising truth about regret is that the path to freedom is not ruminating on our regrets, but instead having what we call a "regret breakout" as we learn to love our regrets and they become a catalyst for growth and change.

If possible, please read chapters 1-2 of Starting Over
before participating in session 1.

ICE BREAKER

Was there ever a time when you simply wanted a do-over? Maybe it was an embarrassing moment or some incident that lives on in infamy among your family or friends. Share this story or incident with the group.

OPENING THOUGHT AND DISCUSSION

1. Regret is a powerful word. When you hear the word regret what comes to mind first?

When we consider our regrets we can place them into one of three large categories or buckets. Read through the descriptions below and discuss the questions that follow.

- **Regrets of Action** - These are things that make us smack our foreheads and say, "Ugh! I wish I'd never . . ." It could be a lie we told, a relationship we torpedoed, a dumb choice we made; the list is endless.

- **Regrets of Inaction** - These are things we wish we would have done, but didn't. It could be opportunities missed, time wasted, risks not taken, and again the list goes on and on.

- **Regrets of Reaction** - Sometimes our greatest regrets start with something that was done to us. It could be abuse, neglect, betrayal, illness, etc. When bad things happen to us, even if it was no fault of our own, we regret them. What can be problematic is what we do in response.

2. What do you think about these categories of regret? Would you say they capture most people's regrets?

3. Which bucket do you think would hold the majority of people's regrets? Which bucket would hold the majority of your regrets?

VIDEO DISCUSSION

Vist www.StartingOverBook.org to watch the video for Session 1.

4. Which part of this "Starting Over" story resonated with you? Explain.

5. How did what you just watched help you better understand what it may mean for you to "Love your regrets?"

BIBLE DISCUSSION

Read Luke 22:54-62 - the story of Peter's denial of Jesus.

54 Then seizing him, they led him away and took him into the house of the high priest. Peter followed at a distance. 55 And when some there had kindled a fire in the middle of the courtyard and had sat down together, Peter sat down with them. 56 A servant girl saw him seated there in the firelight. She looked closely at him and said, "This man was with him."

57 But he denied it. "Woman, I don't know him," he said.

58 A little later someone else saw him and said, "You also are one of them."

"Man, I am not!" Peter replied.

59 About an hour later another asserted, "Certainly this fellow was with him, for he is a Galilean."

60 Peter replied, "Man, I don't know what you're talking about!" Just as he was speaking, the rooster crowed. 61 The Lord turned and looked straight at Peter. Then Peter remembered the word the Lord had spoken to him: "Before the rooster crows today, you will disown me three times." 62 And he went outside and wept bitterly. (Luke 22:54-62)

6. Peter just denied Jesus and immediately regretted the decision he made. In what bucket would you place Peter's regret? Action, Inaction, or Reaction? Explain.

7. Peter acted as a spokesperson and leader of Jesus' disciples, but he disowned Jesus when his life was in danger. What do you suppose he was thinking as the reality of his denial set in?

After Jesus's crucifixion and resurrection, he interacted with his disciples on several occasions. One time Jesus and his disciples had breakfast on the beach where Jesus and Peter sat down to talk.

¹⁵ When they had finished eating, Jesus said to Simon Peter, "Simon son of John, do you love me more than these?"

"Yes, Lord," he said, "you know that I love you."

Jesus said, "Feed my lambs."

¹⁶ Again Jesus said, "Simon son of John, do you love me?"

He answered, "Yes, Lord, you know that I love you."

Jesus said, "Take care of my sheep."

¹⁷ The third time he said to him, "Simon son of John, do you love me?"

Peter was hurt because Jesus asked him the third time, "Do you love me?" He said, "Lord, you know all things; you know that I love you."

Jesus said, "Feed my sheep. ¹⁸ Very truly I tell you, when you were younger you dressed yourself and went where you wanted; but when you are old you will stretch out your hands, and someone else will dress you and lead you where you do not want to go." ¹⁹ Jesus said this to indicate the kind of death by which Peter would glorify God. Then he said to him, "Follow me!" (John 21:15-19)

Peter denied Jesus three times while huddled around a fire in the temple courtyard. Here on the beach Jesus and Peter are huddled around a fire again. This time Jesus asked Peter three times, "Do you love me?" And each time Peter reassures Jesus that he does indeed love him. Jesus's question, "Do you love me?" reassured Peter that their relationship was not over. And his call to "feed my sheep" was a reminder to Peter that Jesus still had a significant purpose in mind for him.

8. How do you think Peter felt as he had this conversation with Jesus? Do you think his feelings changed as Jesus repeatedly asked him, "Do you love me?"

9. Peter went on to be a great leader in the church and remained faithful to the calling he had heard from Jesus during that breakfast around a fire. How do you suppose Peter remembered that breakfast later on in his life?

LIFE APPLICATION

One challenge we may have in learning to live beyond our regrets is our inclination toward rumination. Rumination is when we replay our regret over and over again in our mind, and as a result we get stuck in this repetitive "Sorry Cycle." Like a cow chewing cud, we hash it out again in our mind, and it becomes more than detrimental to our well-being. Clinical Psychologist Melanie Greenberg writes: "Regret can have damaging effects on mind and body when it turns into fruitless rumination and self-blame that keeps people from re-engaging with life. Regret impedes the ability to recover from stressful life events by extending their emotional reach for months, years, or lifetimes."[1]

So instead of ruminating on your regrets in a harmful damaging way, the challenge is to learn to love your regrets. Don't think of regrets as something you try to live without, but let your regrets be a reminder that you can do better! In her very popular TED talk, journalist Kathryn Schulz concludes with this word of advice: "Regret doesn't remind us that we did badly. It reminds us that we know we can do better." Regrets are like feedback on our lives, and if an action, inaction, or reaction has proved harmful, you can learn from it and do better the next time.

10. What are your thoughts on the advice from Kathryn Schultz?

11. In what ways have your own regrets offered important and helpful feedback?

12. What regrets are you continually replaying in your head? How might you, like Peter, begin to learn from your regrets and move beyond them?

---

[1] Melanie Greenberg, "The Psychology of Regret," Psychology Today, May 2012, www.psychologytoday.com/blog/the-mindful-self-express/201205/the-psychology-regret

PERSONAL REFLECTION

The Apostle Paul wrote to Christ-followers in the city of Corinth contrasting "godly sorrow" with "worldly sorrow." These people had committed some actions that were regrettable, and when Paul pointed them out, they felt deeply sorry about it and Paul praises them for their response.

Read 2 Corinthians 7:8-11

[8] *Even if I caused you sorrow by my letter, I do not regret it. Though I did regret it—I see that my letter hurt you, but only for a little while—* [9] *yet now I am happy, not because you were made sorry, but because your sorrow led you to repentance. For you became sorrowful as God intended and so were not harmed in any way by us.* [10] *Godly sorrow brings repentance that leads to salvation and leaves no regret, but worldly sorrow brings death.* [11] *See what this godly sorrow has produced in you: what earnestness, what eagerness to clear yourselves, what indignation, what alarm, what longing, what concern, what readiness to see justice done. At every point you have proved yourselves to be innocent in this matter. (2 Corinthians 7:8-11)*

Worldly Sorrow:[2]
- Is mad about getting caught.
- Justifies sinful behavior.
- Isn't sorry about the pain we've caused another, but just feels bad about ourselves.
- Is me-focused.
- Leads to depression, rebellion, and self-centeredness.

Godly Sorrow:
- Is other – focused.
- Is sorry about the pain caused to another.
- Moves to solve the problem.
- Produces lasting change.
- Is life giving.
- Doesn't leave us feeling condemned.

[2]Material adapted from Henry Cloud & John Townsend, *How People Grow: What the Bible Reveals About Personal Growth.* (Grand Rapids: Zondervan, 2004), 171-173

Think about some of your own regrets. Which of them have moved you to godly sorrow? Which have moved you to worldly sorrow?

Godly Sorrow:

Worldly Sorrow:

One of the ways we escape the "Sorry Cycle" is to tell ourselves a better story. Unfortunately, we too often make negative assumptions about what an event in the past will mean for our future. Here are some ways we replay stories that only serve to keep us in a sorry cycle:

"I hurt my friend so badly that we'll never have a relationship again."

"If I was going to start my own business, I should have done it before I got married and had kids."

"I've tried everything to quit smoking, and it's impossible."

These stories all say, "I'm stuck," and without hope we can believe these stories are the only real possibilities. Now, we must be realistic, but that doesn't mean we should automatically assume the most negative outcomes are inevitable. Instead, we need to learn to consider genuine possibilities. Here are some ways we can predict hopeful and positive results from our stories:

"I hurt my friend badly, but maybe she's ready to forgive me now. I wouldn't be surprised if she misses me as much as I miss her."

"I can't go back and start a business the way I would have before I got married. However, maybe I can follow my entrepreneurial dream in a way that doesn't put

my ability to provide for my family at too much risk."

"I would have been better if I'd never smoked the first cigarette when I was seventeen. But even after years of smoking and numerous failed attempts at quitting, the next time might be the one that succeeds."

What are some negative stories you've told yourself that say, "I'm stuck"?

How can you tell those stories differently, with a hopeful perspective that sees genuine possibility?

A Danish philosopher named Soren Kierkegaard once said, "Life can only be understood backwards, but it must be lived forwards." I think you're ready to see regret, not as something to regret, but as something to love because it is priceless feedback that allows you to better understand your life. I also think you're ready to start moving beyond regret – moving forward in the direction God has for your future.

RECOGNIZE YOUR REGRETS

"Learn to face your regrets head-on!"

Session 2 Big Idea:

If we want to live beyond our regrets we must learn a three-step process for responding constructively to any type of regret. These three steps are: 1) Recognize 2) Release and 3) Redeem your regrets.

The first step in the process is to *recognize* your regrets for what they are. What exactly is it that you are feeling badly about? Have you either underestimated or overestimated how serious it is? What power does it have or not have to affect your future? We need to begin to answer these questions if we want to start over.

If possible, please read chapters 3 of Starting Over
before participating in session 2.

ICE BREAKER

Tell us about a time where you went through a whole day or a party with something glaringly wrong about your outfit or appearance, but no one said anything.

OPENING THOUGHT AND DISCUSSION

Learning to recognize your regrets seems simple enough, doesn't it? Maybe too simple? Yet the human mind has some reflexive responses to powerful emotions - such as regret - that can make it hard to honestly face reality. One unhealthy way of relating to your regrets is to dwell on them and play them over and over again in your mind. Another detrimental way of responding to your regrets is to hide from them. You can do this by denying that there is a problem, distracting yourself with other activities, or simply suppressing your regrets, hoping they will go away. All of these futile attempts keep you trapped in a sorry cycle.

1. Which would you say is the most common way most people avoid dealing with their regrets?

2. What about you? What is your most common "go to" tactic to avoid dealing with your regret?

VIDEO DISCUSSION

Vist www.StartingOverBook.org to watch the video for Session 2.

3. In what ways was Brett honest about his regrets, eventually willing to address them head-on?

4. Why are we often tempted to believe God won't let us start over again?

BIBLE DISCUSSION

King David of Israel once put himself in a situation where he was desperately trying to hide his regretful behavior. You can read the complete story in 2 Samuel 11.

Here is a quick summary of the events leading up to what you will read below:

This regretful situation revolves around David's sin with Bathsheba. He watched her bathe and despite being told she was married, he used his power as king to coerce her into sleeping with him. When she became pregnant, David had her husband killed in battle and he assumed the story was over, that he'd hidden and taken care of this horrible situation. Lust. Adultery. Lying. Murder. Then one of God's prophets, Nathan, who was a friend of David's, came onto the scene.

Read 2 Samuel 12:1-9

The Lord sent Nathan to David. When he came to him, he said, "There were two men in a certain town, one rich and the other poor. ² The rich man had a very large number of sheep and cattle, ³ but the poor man had nothing except one little ewe lamb he had bought. He raised it, and it grew up with him and his children. It shared his food, drank from his cup and even slept in his arms. It was like a daughter to him.

⁴ "Now a traveler came to the rich man, but the rich man refrained from taking one of his own sheep or cattle to prepare a meal for the traveler who had come to him. Instead, he took the ewe lamb that belonged to the poor man and prepared it for the one who had come to him."

⁵ David burned with anger against the man and said to Nathan, "As surely as the Lord lives, the man who did this must die! ⁶ He must pay for that lamb four times over, because he did such a thing and had no pity."

⁷ Then Nathan said to David, "You are the man! This is what the Lord, the God of Israel, says: 'I anointed you king over Israel, and I delivered you from the hand of Saul. 8 I gave your master's house to you, and your master's wives into your arms. I gave you all Israel and Judah. And if all this had been too little, I would have given you even more. 9 Why did you despise the word of the Lord by doing what is evil in his eyes? You struck down Uriah the Hittite with the sword and took his wife to be your own. You killed him with the sword of the Ammonites. (2 Samuel 12:1-9)

5. How do you think David was feeling when Nathan approached him? How do you think Nathan was feeling?

6. How would you say David was hiding his regret? Was it denial? Distraction? Suppression?

7. Just moments after Nathan confronts him, David recognizes his regret and says, *"I have sinned against the Lord."* (2 Samuel 12:13). What is significant about David confessing his sin to Nathan? Why did David say he had "sinned against the Lord"?

LIFE APPLICATION DISCUSSION

8. If someone were to confront you about the regrets you've hidden away, how would you react?

9. Has someone ever acted as a Nathan in your life? How might you encourage one of your close friends to be a "Nathan" to you, by giving him permission to speak into your regrets as Nathan spoke to David?

Each of us has to face our regrets head-on! Like David, our first step is likely to crawl out of the darkness and face what has happened. It isn't easy, but it is always necessary. You can't change what happened in the past, but you can change how you respond to it in the future.

10. Take a quick look at the Personal Reflection time at the end of this session. This exercise is important, but hard work. Will you commit to doing it? How can each of you be an encouragement to one another this week?

PERSONAL REFLECTION

You may think you know your regrets well enough; after all you've been living with them for a long time! However, even though your regrets may be painful to you, it doesn't mean you've looked at them as carefully as you need to in order to recognize them for what they really are.

So take some time to assess what went wrong in your life. It might help you to think about this as a process of interviewing yourself. What follows are a few recommendations and some questions you can ask of yourself so you can recognize your regrets and assign to them their appropriate place in your life story.

A few recommendations:

1. Take some time to be alone with God. Ask God to guide you through this process.

2. Don't be afraid of your emotions. If you become emotional it's OK to cry or be angry.

3. If you think it would be beneficial to talk this out with another person, find a close friend or family member.

4. You may even consider making an appointment with a therapist or spiritual mentor, advisor, or director.

EMBRACE THE TRUTH

1. Is your regret one of action, inaction, or reaction?

2. Who was involved?

3. What happened?

4. When did it happen?

5. Where did it happen?

6. Why did it happen?

7. How did it happen?

8. What is the right label for what happened?

9. How big of a deal was it, really? Remember you could be assigning too little importance or not enough to what has happened?

10. What is its lasting impact? How have you been affected mentally, spiritually, and emotionally?

11. How are others hurting because of this?

TAKE FROM IT WHAT YOU CAN

In order to break free from the Sorry Cycle, we have to mine our experiences for whatever they can teach us. This is more than information gathering regarding our regrets; we are also need to put them in perspective so we know what to do with them. What can your regrets teach you about what you need to do more of, do less of, or do differently in the future?

12. What could you do more of in the future?

13. What could you do less of in the future?

14. What could you do differently in the future?

ACTION STEP

What's your next step in recognizing your regrets? Are you still struggling with denial, distraction, or suppression? Do you need to talk to someone about it? Or are you ready to clearly analyze what happened, admit your part in it, and move onto step 2? Write down your action steps and pray about them.

RELEASE YOUR REGRETS

"Learn to let go of your regrets"

Session 3 Big Idea:

When we have done something wrong or when something undeserved has happened to us, we can easily get hung up in guilt, blame, and grudge holding. The questions and emotions inside us can prevent us from moving past our regrets in a new direction. Once we recognize our regrets, it's time to begin to release them. This is a critical step that often demands that we forgive or seek forgiveness moving us one step closer to breaking out of thew Sorry Cycle. So if regret has become a useless burden around your neck, drop it. Let's learn to let it go. Release it.

If possible, please read chapter 4 of Starting Over
before participating in session 3.

ICE BREAKER

If you could take a time machine into the past to warn a historical character before they made a regretful decision, whom would you pick? Explain.

OPENING THOUGHTS AND DISCUSSION

If we are to release regret we have to do the hard work of looking at our lives and answering some tough questions about our regrets.

1.   When you hear the phrase "release regret," what picture does that paint in your mind?

2.   Why do we have a tendency to hold on to our regrets?

VIDEO DISCUSSION

Vist www.StartingOverBook.org to watch the video for Session 3.

3.   What part of Brett's starting over story did you find most helpful to you?

4.   What role did forgiveness play in Brett's story? How are you beginning to see that forgiveness will play an important part in your starting over story?

BIBLE DISCUSSION

In our last session we looked at the story of King David of Israel. David had been walking on the roof of his palace when he looked down and saw Bathsheba bathing. The text says she was very beautiful and David desired her. He called her to his room and committed adultery with her. When he found out later that Bathsheba was pregnant he had her husband, Uriah, killed. Nathan the prophet confronted David and when David realized he had been found out he confessed to Nathan what he had done.

David was famous for loving God. He was called "the man after God's own heart." He was the warrior who stared down a giant calling out, "The battle is the Lord's!" He worshipped God with such abandon it made other people despise him. He wrote many meaningful songs of spiritual depth. Now, he was exposed as an adulterer and a murder.

What did he do next? David did what he had done in moments of distress and situations of powerful emotion ever since he was a youth. He picked up his harp, headed for a place of solitude, and strummed out his feelings of guilt and sorrow before God. The song David wrote on that occasion is recorded in Psalm 51.

As you read through the Psalm, underline the words
and phrases that stand out to you.

Psalm 51

1   *Have mercy on me, O God,*
   according to your unfailing love;
according to your great compassion
   blot out my transgressions.
2 *Wash away all my iniquity*
   and cleanse me from my sin.
3 *For I know my transgressions,*
   and my sin is always before me.
4 *Against you, you only, have I sinned*
   and done what is evil in your sight;
so you are right in your verdict
   and justified when you judge.
5 *Surely I was sinful at birth,*
   sinful from the time my mother conceived me.
6 *Yet you desired faithfulness even in the womb;*
   you taught me wisdom in that secret place.
7 *Cleanse me with hyssop, and I will be clean;*
   wash me, and I will be whiter than snow.
8 *Let me hear joy and gladness;*
   let the bones you have crushed rejoice.
9 *Hide your face from my sins*
   and blot out all my iniquity.
10 *Create in me a pure heart, O God,*
   and renew a steadfast spirit within me.
11 *Do not cast me from your presence*
   or take your Holy Spirit from me.
12 *Restore to me the joy of your salvation*
   and grant me a willing spirit, to sustain me.

5. What words and phrases stand out to you most in Psalm 51? Explain.

6. In what ways do you see David recognizing and releasing his regrets in this song?

7. Can you relate to David? How has God helped you release a regret and come out on the other side closer to Him?

LIFE APPLICATION

David confessed his sin and released his regrets and asked for God's forgiveness. It was then that the prophet Nathan came to him and announced that the Lord had taken away David's sin.[1]

8. The process of letting go of our regrets is usually tied to forgiveness. Is it harder for you to receive forgiveness from others, extend it to others, or forgive yourself? How would you go about letting go of a regret that may be the result of a life circumstance?

---

[1] 2 Samuel 12:13

9. Lewis Smedes wrote that when we forgive, "You set a prisoner free, but you discover that the real prisoner was yourself."[2] In what ways can forgiving someone else set you free from regret?

10. God wants you to be free. God gave us his Son, Jesus, so all of us might experience forgiveness and freedom. What do you need to let go of to truly be free?

PERSONAL REFLECTION

Once we have recognized our regrets we can begin to release them. Use these five questions to help you begin the process of releasing your regret.

1. **Do you regret committing a sin?** Your regret was not just a failure, it was something you did that put distance between you and God. Letting go of that regret will require repentance and proceeding in a different direction. Repentance is relational. Repentance leads to forgiveness and brings you back into a closer relationship with God.

2. **Do you regret hurting someone else?** If your regret is the result of hurt you caused to someone else, you have to do your best to bring healing to the wound you've inflicted. If possible, apologize to the person and ask forgiveness. If there are circumstances that make this impossible, you have to forgive yourself and pray that reconciliation may be possible later.

[2]Lewis B. Smedes. Forgive and Forget: Healing the Hurts We Don't Deserve (San Francisco: HarperOne 1996), 131.

3. **Do you regret a mistake you made?** Sometimes we have made a tactical blunder or committed an error in judgment, but it wasn't a sin. It was an honest mistake or accident. So we don't need to ask God's forgiveness for it. We need to let ourselves off the hook. Remind yourself that it is something to learn from, not something to torment yourself over.

4. **Do you regret being hurt by someone else?** If somebody else has done something wrong to you, the answer is easy – forgive him or her. Easy to say, that is. Often hard to do. Sometimes the deeds that have been done to us were unbelievably cruel and hurtful. And honestly it might take awhile before we get to a point where we're genuinely ready to forgive.

5. **Do you regret pain you feel from life circumstances?** You develop a chronic illness. A hurricane sweeps away your home. Sometimes there is no one to blame for the regret you feel. It's merely life's circumstances that have caused your regret. Here is a word of caution: resist the temptation to blame God. He is never the author of evil. He grieves right alongside you, and he wants you to share with him how you are feeling.

EXERCISING YOUR "RELEASE" MUSCLES

Now that you've taken the first steps in releasing your regrets, you might be tempted to go about your life as usual. Releasing regrets can be like a person who decides to get a gym membership, but then doesn't actually go to the gym. Don't make that mistake as you begin to release your regrets. Start practicing as soon as possible. Ask for forgiveness. Extend forgiveness to others. Forgive yourself. Use the following methods for building your "release muscles."

HAVE A CONVERSATION

Whether you've hurt someone or someone has hurt you, you will more than likely need to have a conversation to find resolution in the relationship. If you ask for forgiveness or grant it to someone else, that will help you release your regrets. There may be times when a conversation with someone is not possible. The apostle Paul must have realized this when he wrote these words: "If it is possible, as far as it depends on you, live at peace with everyone. (Romans 12:18)

WRITE A LETTER

Sometimes a conversation won't work, because the other party is no longer living or they are unwilling to meet or speak with you. Sometimes the situation between you and the other party might only be made worse through further contact. In cases like these, write a letter, putting all your thoughts down about what happened. Don't hold back and write what comes into your mind. You aren't actually going to send the letter to the other party, but the process of putting your thoughts and emotions down on paper will be helpful to you in releasing your regrets.

PRAY

Another option available to us is prayer. Talk to God about the regrets you have bottled up inside of you. Ask God to help you forgive yourself, forgive someone who hurt you, and even seek reconciliation if that's possible. The Bible says to pray for our enemies, so pray for the good of those who have hurt you. Be honest with God in prayer and see if it doesn't lead to an attitude of surrender as you come to peace with what has happened in the past.

REDEEM YOUR REGRETS

"A mistake turned into a miracle."

Session 4 Big Idea:

To exit the Sorry Cycle and start over, first we must recognize our regret and then we release it. The third step in the process is best described by the term redeem. No other word so richly defines the way we break free from regret and move ahead. We need to allow God to redeem our regrets, trusting him to bring something good out of them.

If we let him, God will redeem our regrets. This step, unlike the previous two, is not about anything we can do. Rather, this is only something that God can do when we humble ourselves to bring our regrets to him so he can make something beautiful out of them. "He works all things for good . . . " (Romans 8:28).

If possible, please read chapter 5 of Starting Over before participating in session 4.

ICE BREAKER

What is one food you hated as a child, but have grown to like as an adult?

OPENING THOUGHT AND DISCUSSION

In this session we are talking about redeeming our regrets. Redemption is what happens when unexpected good comes out of a situation that you could only expect to result in something bad. We could call this the long view of our mistakes. One helpful way of understanding redemption is to think back to the days when you could take an empty useless Coca-Cola bottle and exchange it for 10 cents, and then turn around and buy a brand new pack of baseball cards. How awesome was that! You could redeem an old useless bottle for a pack of baseball cards!

1. When have you seen unexpected good come from a situation when you could only have expected something bad?

2. Why is it so hard to have a long view of our regrets?

VIDEO DISCUSSION

Vist www.StartingOverBook.org to watch the video for Session 4.

3. What is God doing to redeem Brett's regret? What role is Brett playing in that redemption?

4. How hopeful are you that God could redeem your regret? Explain.

BIBLE DISCUSSION

The word redemption is a significant theological word that we may not use everyday, but it's an idea many of us know or have experienced. In the New Testament, one of the words that is translated "redemption" is the Greek word lytrosis, and it was frequently used to mean redeem, liberate, ransom, or set free. This word was often used in reference to the purchase of a slave's freedom. A slave was "redeemed" when the price or ransom was paid for his freedom.

Here are a few places where lytrosis appears in the New Testament:

- *"For even the Son of Man did not come to be served, but to serve, and to give his life as a ransom for many." (Mark 10:45)*

- *"[He] gave himself for us to redeem us from all wickedness and to purify for himself a people that are his very own, eager to do what is good." (Titus 2:14)*

- *"For there is one God and one mediator between God and mankind, the man Christ Jesus, who gave himself as a ransom for all people." (1 Timothy 2:5-6)*

5. How would you summarize what these verses are saying regarding redemption?

6. How do these verses speak to the truth that Jesus wants to redeem us, even our regrets?

7. In Titus 2:14 we read that Jesus gave himself up for us so we would be purified, eager to do what is good. How might holding onto our regrets keep us from being eager to do what is good?

In Session 2 we looked at the life of David and how he made several regretful decisions. He had an adulterous affair with Uriah's wife, and when she was found to be pregnant, he had her husband killed. Even so, David confessed his sin to God and asked for God's forgiveness, and David and Bathsheba went on to have a son together named Solomon. He is remembered as a great king and is mentioned in the genealogy of Jesus in Matthew 1. Despite the ugliness of his sin and the regret he may have felt, God redeemed his story by weaving it into the story of Jesus.

8. Why are we tempted to believe that some regrets are beyond God's power to redeem?

LIFE APPLICATION

The philosopher, Dallas Willard once said, "Nothing irredeemable has happened or can happen to us on our way to our destiny in God's full world."[1] That statement was his way of explaining Romans 8:28: *"And we know that in all things God works for the good of those who love him, who have been called according to his purpose."*

9. What have you written off as irredeemable in your own life? What would it take for you to begin to see it through the eyes of Romans 8:28?

---

[1]Dallas Willard, *The Divine Conspiracy: Rediscovering Our Hidden Life In God* (New York: Harper Collins 2009), 337.

In the book Starting Over, Jon & Dave Ferguson encourage us to take preparatory steps so God can work his redemption in our lives. For example, if you are desiring a more challenging or fulfilling career, perhaps it's time to go back to school or explore additional training of some kind.

10. What do think about the notion of taking preparatory steps so God can work redemption in our lives?

11. What are some preparatory steps you can take to give God more room to work his redemptive ways with your regrets?

12. The first two steps in starting over are recognizing and releasing our regrets. The third step, redeeming our regrets, is different than the other two, because it something only God can do. On a scale of 1 to 10 with 1 being incredibly impatient and 10 having the patience of a saint how difficult is it for you to "wait on God" to redeem your regrets?

PERSONAL REFLECTION

The Faces of Redemption

The way God redeems your regrets may look different from the way God redeems someone else's regrets. They can be as different as each one of our faces. Each time God redeems someone's difficult situation or pain, it is perfectly adapted for him or her. While this list isn't exhaustive, your own redemption might look a bit like one of the following:

Redemption can look like finding your way back to God.
Many people take treacherous detours in life before they find themselves considering questions of spiritual depth. Then when they take a second look at God they realize God has been waiting for them all this time with open arms.

Redemption can look like spiritual growth.
Sometimes when the bottom of our lives fall out, we realize we haven't been following God as closely as we thought, and we turn back to him and grow in ways we never thought possible.

Redemption can look like rescheduling.
Maybe your well-laid plans did come through for your business or your family, but in the end the way things worked out turned out better than what you originally planned.

Redemption can look like blessing
One character in the Bible named Job, loses everything, but by the end of the story is blessed in ways he never dreamed possible. Sometimes we go through periods of intense suffering. And even though God may not take the pain away and leave us with many questions, we experience unexpected goodness and blessing in our lives,

Redemption can look like a chance to bless others.
This may happen when alcoholics or drug addicts get sober and then help others find sobriety as well. Redemption can take the form of a gift of service to others. It's like God has said, *"Help others with what you have learned in your hard times."*

13. As you look at the different "Faces of Redemption," which of these align most closely with the redemption you are seeking or have seen God work in your life?

If you are ready to trust God to redeem your regret, say these words to him in prayer: "God, you know what happened that has caused me so much regret. I have done everything I can to release that regret and experience forgiveness. Now I ask you to do what only you can do: make good come from this regret. Turn the dark into light. I give this to you, dear God. Amen.

LIVING BEYOND YOUR REGRETS

"Starting over every day."

Session 5 Big Idea:

You can live beyond regrets permanently. The starting over process is not just a one-time fix, but rather a skill you can retain (like riding a bike) and employ whenever you need it. When something goes wrong in life – and of course that will continue to happen – you can recover your momentum quickly and keep moving forward. Living beyond regrets can become a way of life.

Once you have learned to move beyond a regret using the three R's – Recognize, Release, and Redeem – you can apply that same method to future regrets. You will develop the instinct of reacting to regret as quickly as possible by recognizing it, releasing it, and redeeming it. This way you don't get stuck in a Sorry Cycle. Instead you can rotate around the Starting Over Loop and get on with your life. No more endless cycles around and around. It can be one and done through the loop. This is your life beyond regrets!

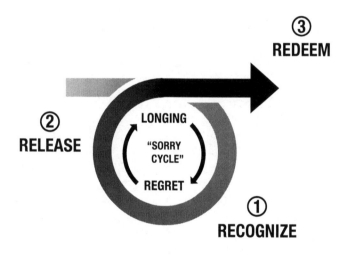

If possible, please read chapter 11 of Starting Over before participating in session 5.

ICE BREAKER

What is one life-long skill or hobby that you seem to be able to pick up as if you never let it go no matter how long it's been since you actually practiced it (and you can't say ride a bicycle!)?

OPENING THOUGHT AND DISCUSSION

The Starting Over Loop is a discipline you develop when you learn to recognize, release, and redeem your regrets. Talk about the Starting Over Loop together until each of you has a clear understanding of it, because you will need to recall it the moment you need it.

1. As you look at the Starting Over Loop, what are your initial thoughts?

2. How would your life look different if you could practice the Starting Over Loop with your regrets?

3. Which do you think is the most difficult step in the Starting Over Loop? Explain.

VIDEO DISCUSSION

Vist www.StartingOverBook.org to watch the video for Session 5.

4. How did this "Starting Over" story encourage or challenge you?

5. Which aspect of the Starting Over Loop is still unclear to you? Explain

BIBLE DISCUSSION

One of the earliest and most important Christian leaders was a man named Paul. However, before he was a faithful follower of Jesus he attacked and killed followers of Jesus, because he thought he was doing right by his religious heritage. Everything changed when he had an encounter with Jesus where he literally turns his life around and chooses to follow Jesus ("the Way"), himself. Through the power of God's grace he was able to receive forgiveness, ask for forgiveness from others, and forgive himself. Read his story below from Acts 22.

I persecuted the followers of this Way to their death, arresting both men and women and throwing them into prison, 5 as the high priest and all the Council can themselves testify. I even obtained letters from them to their associates in Damascus, and went there to bring these people as prisoners to Jerusalem to be punished.

6 "About noon as I came near Damascus, suddenly a bright light from heaven flashed around me. 7 I fell to the ground and heard a voice say to me, 'Saul! Saul! Why do you persecute me?'

8 "'Who are you, Lord?' I asked.

" 'I am Jesus of Nazareth, whom you are persecuting,' he replied. 9 My companions saw the light, but they did not understand the voice of him who was speaking to me.

10 "'What shall I do, Lord?' I asked.

" 'Get up,' the Lord said, 'and go into Damascus. There you will be told all that you have been assigned to do.' 11 My companions led me by the hand into Damascus, because the brilliance of the light had blinded me.

12 "A man named Ananias came to see me. He was a devout observer of the law and highly respected by all the Jews living there. 13 He stood beside me and said, 'Brother Saul, receive your sight!' And at that very moment I was able to see him.

14 "Then he said: 'The God of our ancestors has chosen you to know his will and to see the Righteous One and to hear words from his mouth. 15 You will be his witness to all people of what you have seen and heard. 16 And now what are you waiting for? Get up, be baptized and wash your sins away, calling on his name.'

6. How do you think Paul felt the moment he realized he was wrong about Jesus and his followers?

7. God gave Paul a chance to start over despite the severity of his sins. Paul even calls himself the worst of sinners (1 Timothy 1:15). What does that say about God if he can forgive even the "worst of sinners?"

8. How did God redeem even Paul's deepest regrets, using them for ultimate good and to help others find their way back to God?

9. Why do you think Paul spoke so openly about his past regrets? Do you think you could have that same courage and transparency? Explain.

10. Ananias was the personal connection Paul needed in order to Start Over. Do you have someone like Ananias in your life, who speaks the truth in love to you and can help you continue to walk through the Starting Over Loop?

LIFE APPLICATION

11. What are some common excuses that keep us from walking through the Starting Over Loop?

12. How does Paul's story inspire or encourage you to live beyond your regrets?

13. What steps do you need to take in order to make the Starting Over Loop a regular part of how you deal with life's deepest regrets?

CLOSING REFLECTION

Through a process of starting over we can put our regrets behind us. They lose their power to a point where they no longer pose obstacles to growth and forward motion. That's an amazing thing. But how awesome would it be if those regrets could be erased entirely? And that's just what's going to happen one day! For those who have found their way back to God, we have a new existence coming. It's an eternal life that knows no regret.

Revelation 21:3-4 talks about that new existence in this way: "And I heard a loud voice from the throne saying, "Look! God's dwelling place is now among the people, and he will dwell with them. They will be his people, and God himself will be with them and be their God. ⁴He will wipe every tear from their eyes. There will be no more death or mourning or crying or pain, for the old order of things has passed away." (Revelation 21:3-4)

PERSONAL REFLECTION

If you're still having trouble getting past your regrets try to reevaluate how you are engaging the Starting Over Loop. It may be that you are getting hung up in an area where you need to ask some more hard questions.

Instead of recognizing regret, are you turning a blind eye to it?

Sometimes we can be afraid of the pain that comes with regret. Asking hard questions and recognizing your regrets can cause a lot of pain. It is like touching a wound. Yet there is something critical in analyzing your regrets that can actually begin drain it of the pain it may be causing you. Be willing to risk the short-term pain for the long-term reward that will follow.

Instead of releasing your regret, are you holding on to it?

Our feelings about regrets can sometimes get turned upside down. You may end up holding onto regrets because you are too mad at the world, at God, or at a single person to let it go. You may even feel like it is your duty to hang onto that anger, or you may not be sure who you would be if the regret no longer had such a strong hold on you. The goal is to love your regrets as events from your past that can prove instructive for the future, not as present experiences your willing to give control of your life.

Instead of redeeming your regret, are you resisting redemption?

To receive redemption from God we need to have a posture of openness to what he will bring. Instead, though, we can become closed off to his work. Maybe you've stopped looking to the future, and are focused on the regret in the past. Instead of waiting for God, you may not be giving him the time of day.

If so, why is this happening?

Do you trust God? If so, try recalling the promises God makes in Scripture. If God was faithful then can you trust in him to be faithful to you today? Second, remember what he's done in the lives of others again and again to redeem their regrets.

If you are having trouble believing or trusting God, try practicing this simple prayer called out by a father asking Jesus to heal his son in Mark 9:24: I do believe; help me overcome my unbelief.

CONCLUDING REFLECTIONS

The following verses are taken from Lamentations 3:19 – 26. They envision a strong military man who has just come from the battle where Jerusalem has fallen to the Babylonians. The backdrop to the story is that Israel has been unfaithful to God, and so God has allowed the Babylonians to conquer Jerusalem. And amidst the pain and regret this strong military man chokes out these words:

> I remember my affliction and my wandering,
>   the bitterness and the gall.
> I well remember them,
>   and my soul is downcast within me.
> Yet this I call to mind
>   and therefore I have hope:
> Because of the Lord's great love we are not consumed,
>   for his compassions never fail.
> They are new every morning;
>   great is your faithfulness.
> I say to myself, "The Lord is my portion;
>   therefore I will wait for him."
> The Lord is good to those whose hope is in him,
>   to the one who seeks him;
> it is good to wait quietly
>   for the salvation of the Lord.

Did you hear that? God's compassion is new every morning! That means every day is another chance to start over! Wait on the Lord; trust in him and see that he is faithful. You won't be sorry! Over time you'll notice those regrets in the rearview mirror getting smaller and smaller. They will lose their power to a point where they no longer pose obstacles to forward motion and growth. That's an amazing thing. But don't forget, God has promised that all our regrets will one day be permanently erased. For all those who have found their way back to God, we've got a new existence coming. It's an eternal life that knows no regret.

LOVE
YOUR REGRETS

SESSION 1 LEADER'S GUIDE

Objective: To help participants see how our regrets can give us helpful feedback. We don't have to ruminate on them, but can let them be reminders that with God's help we can do better.

What you need for this session:
- At least one copy of the book *Starting Over* to refer to if needed.
- Access to this session's video at www.StartingOverBook.org
- A laptop, television, or monitor where the whole group can watch.
- A Bible for yourself and for other participants.
- Index cards and pens or pencils.

Icebreaker
Welcome the members of the group to the first session. Strike up a friendly conversation with the group and keep the examples light-hearted and fun.

Opening thought and discussion
The topic of regret is very personal and each person is probably carrying a variety of regrets, some more deeply felt than others. Don't press in too much with these opening questions. You simply want people to thinking analytically about regret before they begin to reflect on specific regrets of their own.

Video Discussion
After playing the video, use these questions to help the group reflect on what they just watched.

Bible Discussion
Use these questions to help people see that one of the greatest leaders in the early church messed up really bad and had deep regrets. However, Jesus continued to offer him hope with a chance to start over.

Life Application Discussion

Your group may be reluctant to share very much of their story this first evening. On the other hand, there may be some that get emotional even thinking about regrets. Go slow; be ready for tears or bitterness. It may be that the group is only ready to talk about some basic, surface regrets. No matter what kind of regrets are shared, try to encourage the group to see the potential our regrets have to give us feedback as we start over with God's help. If you have a larger group it may be helpful to break into two or more smaller groups, so people feel more comfortable sharing and have a greater chance to talk.

Closing Prayer

Lead the prayer asking God to help everyone in the group learn to see their regrets as reminders that with his help we can start over.

Preview of the Next Session

Encourage everyone to work through the personal reflection section of the participant's guide. It will help them to process their regrets and be in a position of greater openness to next week's session, where we will look at the beginning of the three-step process to live beyond our regrets.

LEADER'S GUIDE SESSION 2

RECOGNIZE YOUR REGRETS

SESSION 2 LEADER'S GUIDE

Objective: To help participants begin to recognize their regrets as honestly as they can. When we are open and honest with ourselves our regrets lose their power to shape our future.

What you need for this session:
- At least one copy of the book *Starting Over* to refer to if needed.
- Access to this session's video at www.StartingOverBook.org
- A laptop, television, or monitor where the whole group can watch.
- A Bible for yourself and for other participants.
- Index cards and pens or pencils..

Icebreaker
Use this icebreaker to set the tone before you ease into the discussion about recognizing your regrets.

Opening thought and discussion
Use these questions to get people thinking about the fact that we can deal with our regret in some unhealthy ways. Helping people see this through hypothetical examples is fine since some people may not want to get too personal initially. Don't press in too much on the second question; be patient with people. They will open up when they feel safe and ready to share.

Video Discussion
Use these questions to further explore the topic and help the group reflect on what they just watched.

Bible Discussion
Use these questions to help people see that once David was exposed he doesn't try to hide his sin and regret. As king, he could have had Nathan thrown into prison or killed, but he doesn't. He confesses his sin and asks for forgiveness (Psalm 51).

Life Application Discussion

Use these questions to get people thinking about their own need to face their regrets head-on. The members of your group are going to need others around them to speak into their lives if they are truly going to start over. The personal reflection time for the week is really important, so encourage the group to make time to complete that work. Then ask the group to encourage one another this week to finish the work.

Before they leave, have them set up a way to connect between sessions. It could be a quick email, text, phone call, or meeting over coffee. If people are afraid of being honest about their regrets they will need loving people who offer encouragement and support. Your group can help with the beginning of that process.

Closing Prayer

End your group time by thanking God for his grace and praying for everyone in the group to have the courage to face their regrets head-on in the coming week. If group members are comfortable, ask each person to say a brief prayer for the person on their right.

Preview of the Next Session

Encourage the group to do the personal reflection. Tell the group something like this, "It will take a little more effort, but I know it will pay off in the long run. I'm looking forward to seeing you next week. We'll be looking at how God's forgiveness can help us release our regrets."

LEADER'S GUIDE SESSION 3

RELEASE YOUR REGRETS

SESSION 3 LEADER'S GUIDE

Objective: To help participants see that forgiveness is vital to the starting over process. The members of your group may need to receive forgiveness from God or extend forgiveness to others or forgive themselves.

What you need for this session:
- At least one copy of the book *Starting Over* to refer to if needed.
- Access to this session's video at www.StartingOverBook.org
- A laptop, television, or monitor where the whole group can watch.
- A Bible for yourself and for other participants.
- Index cards and pens or pencils.

Icebreaker
Use this question to warm people up to the discussion. This should be fun and easy for everyone to answer.

Opening thought and discussion
Use these questions to get your group thinking about what it takes to do something challenging. This can be anything from running a race to sticking to a diet to getting up earlier in the morning. The idea here is to set the table for people to realize that releasing your regrets is also very challenging.

Video Discussion
Use these questions to further explore the topic and help the group reflect on what they just watched

Bible Discussion
Use these questions to help the group see how David recognized and released his regrets. Pay special attention to the themes of forgiveness and confession.

Life Application Discussion

Use these questions to get people thinking about the ways they need to receive or extend forgiveness. Encourage the group to be honest with their struggle to forgive. It's hard, challenging work that goes beyond saying the words, "I forgive you." Help the group see that as they begin to release regrets it will get easier to give and receive forgiveness.

Closing Prayer

Finish your time together by thanking God for his forgiveness. Pray that everyone in the group would know God's love and forgiveness and be able to show that to others. In addition, consider asking each person to write on an index card how he or she would like for the group to pray for him or her. Then pass the cards out to the group members, asking them to keep that person's prayer request in mind this upcoming week.

Preview of the Next Session

Encourage the group to complete the personal reflection time. Let them know the following week will be the third and final step of learning to live beyond regret. It is the part where we ask God to step in and do what only God can do. Let them know they can't truly live beyond regrets without this step.

REDEEM YOUR REGRETS

SESSION 4 LEADER'S GUIDE

Objective: To help participants trust God to redeem their regrets. Help your group think about the preparatory steps they can take towards the redemption God wants to work in their lives.

What you need for this session:
- At least one copy of the book *Starting Over* to refer to if needed.
- Access to this session's video at www.StartingOverBook.org
- A laptop, television, or monitor where the whole group can watch.
- A Bible for yourself and for other participants.
- Index cards and pens or pencils.

Icebreaker

Use this question to get people laughing about weird or exotic food they would never eat again. This helps people see, albeit in a small way, how even silly regrets can become a funny story or memory. This hints at the larger truth about how God wants to redeem our entire lives, even our regrets.

Opening thought and discussion

Use these questions to get people thinking about the concept of redemption. If people are struggling to get the concept, be ready to share some of your own examples or stories of redemption you've seen or experienced firsthand.

Video Discussion

Use these questions to further explore the topic and help the group reflect on what they just watched

Bible Discussion
Use these questions to help people see that God wants to redeem all of us. He wants to buy us all back. Don't miss the opportunity to help people see the truth in the Titus passage. If we don't let God redeem our regrets, and instead let our regrets maintain their hold over us, we will struggle to be people who are "eager to do what is good," because we will be consumed with our own Sorry Cycle.

Life Application Discussion
Use these questions to get the members of the group thinking about ways they can take small steps in trusting God. There is an example in the guide to get people's creative juices flowing.

Closing Prayer
If you're group is ready for this, ask them to break into pairs for the closing prayer. Then encourage them to pray for each other, asking God to help one another take new steps in learning to trust God more. Also challenge them ask God to redeem each other's regrets as only he can.

Preview of the Next Session
Next week is the final week and it will help everyone see how to live life beyond regrets. Not only that, it will help them see how they can encourage others to escape the Sorry Cycle. This final session brings it all home and ties all the weeks together. They won't want to miss it.

LIVING BEYOND REGRETS

SESSION 5 LEADER'S GUIDE

Objective: To help participants see how they can live beyond regret permanently. Help the group see that once they learn how to walk thru the Starting Over Loop they can put it into practice any time regrets come along.

What you need for this session:
- At least one copy of the book *Starting Over* to refer to if needed.
- Access to this session's video at www.StartingOverBook.org
- A laptop, television, or monitor where the whole group can watch.
- A Bible for yourself and for other participants.
- Index cards and pens or pencils.

Icebreaker
Use this question to loosen people up to the topic and feel free to make comparisons between life long skills and the Starting Over Loop.

Opening thought and discussion
Make sure everyone in the group fully understands how the three R's (Recognize, Release, and Redeem) work together to help us live beyond regret. This understanding will help them through the remainder of the session and hopefully the rest of their lives.

Video Discussion
Use these questions to further explore the topic and help the group reflect on what they just watched.

Bible Discussion
These questions will highlight Paul as the self-proclaimed "worst of sinners". If any members of the group feel as if their situation is beyond redemption, point out Paul's story. If God can redeem Paul's story, why can't he redeem yours?

Life Application Discussion

Use these questions to push through any remaining excuses people may have. Get them to imagine their life without regret. You may need to press the group to formulate some action steps. Ask them questions about how they will stick to their plan or how they will remain accountable. Maybe your small group continues to offer the necessary support. Perhaps you can recommend some next steps for anyone in the group still struggling with what to do next such as seeking a professional therapist, spiritual coach or mentor.

Closing Prayer

End your group time with a prayer. Encourage group members to offer a brief prayer of thanks for what God has done in and through them over the course of these discussions. Also pray that God would help each person take the necessary steps to continue live a life without regrets and to help others do the same.

....

STARTING OVER NOTES

STARTING OVER NOTES

STARTING OVER NOTES

STARTING OVER NOTES

STARTING OVER NOTES

STARTING OVER NOTES

STARTING OVER NOTES

STARTING OVER NOTES

STARTING OVER NOTES

STARTING OVER NOTES

STARTING OVER NOTES

Made in the USA
Middletown, DE
08 July 2017